Deadly Poetry

Deadly Poetry

Marlene Mesot

Print layout, e–book conversion, and cover design
by DLD Books

DLD Books

www.dldbooks.com
Editing and Self–Publishing Services

ISBN: 979-8-9858477-2-7

4 Elements
of Mystery Series

1. The Purging Fire
2. The Snowball Effect
3. Whirlwind of Fear
4. Terra Terror

More Mysteries

The Cat Stalker's Sonnets — novel

Poetry

Edgy Poetry
Deadly Poetry
The Author's Edge

www.marlsmenagerie.com

For the wages of sin is death, but the free gift of God is
eternal life in Christ Jesus our Lord.

Romans 6:23
New American Standard Bible

Table of Contents

Deadly Poetry Introduction
(Couplet)
04/07/2021

You need no instruction,
For a deadly poetry introduction.

These are poems of death.
Put it to the test.

If each poem starts with one word,
It is not too absurd.

Shorter heightens action,
To your satisfaction.

More than edgy I confess,
These are creepy at best.

These are not poems of horror,
Merely food for fodder.

Consider this a warning,
If you are in mourning.

What Is Life About?
(Trident)
10/19/2021

Can we figure out,
What is life about?
Do we want to know?

The tide comes in,
The tide goes out.
Unwavering,

To and fro,
Ebb and flow,
Life tosses.

Life
(Quatrain)
10/06/2021

This is not a quiz.
Is this all there is?
From this life you take,
What of life you make?

Present becomes past.
How long does it last?
Future sight unseen.
Nothing seems serene.

What is Heaven for?
To admire, adore?
Is there such a place?
Don't dismiss in haste.

What do you believe?
What does faith achieve?
Is this all there is?
Life is not a quiz.

Alliteration

(Quatrain)

04/08/2021

Creepy, crawly,
Squirmy, squally,
Unknown things,
Fear brings.

Gritty, grimy,
Feeling slimy,
Slithering unknown,
Chilling to the bone.

The phenomenon of death,
Yet unknown at best,
Remains a mystery,
Adds insecurity.

Death
(Acrostic)
04/07/2021

Distilled
Everlasting
Alluring
Timeless
Hauntingly unknown

Death Trek

(Quatrain)

(04/28/2021)

Some see death as the end,
Some see it as just a bend
In the fabric of our existence,
Where there is no resistance.

Some see reincarnation as a constant climb,
Toward reaching existence of the Divine.
Some see death as being final,
With nothing more definable.

But what if it is eternal separation,
Would there then be trepidation?
What if it is complete aloneness?
Each of us treks his/her own soulfulness.

Experience

(Quatrain)

04/07/2021

Six of one,
Half dozen of another,
Death is an experience,
Unlike any other.

What is life to say?
Does inner spirit dwell?
No human has a sway.
Can we really tell?

Experience there is none.
This surely is no fun.
Pondering this mess—
The certainty of death.

Steady as a rock,
The finality of death,
Ticking like a clock,
Will it be a rest?

One thing now is certain,
No one sees beyond the curtain.
No one knows its effect.
No one comes back from death.

Opposites
(Quatrain)
04/07/2021

Like this and that,
Opposites attract.
Balance good and bad.
Adjust yourself a tad.

Darkness should seek light.
Weakness needs some might.
Left and right both true.
Male and female two.

Are we all one kind?
Or is this sentiment blind?
Is death opposite life?
Who will wield the knife?

Impressions
(Quatrain)
10/22/2021

Ashes to ashes,
Dust to dust,
How to remember,
Each of us.

What effect has a life,
On this earth?
What impact does it have?
Measure girth.

What is it worth,
Tangled web,
To stay on this earth,
Without dread?

Where does it end?
Life unfolds.
No longer kin.
When we're old.

Weather

(Quatrain)

04/07/2021

Weather dark and dreary,
Makes the old bones weary.
When broken parts ache,
Bad weather, no mistake.

Storm clouds in the sky,
Set our fears on high.
Rain and snow are treacherous.
Treat them both as dangerous.

Accidents in bad weather,
Make us stick together.
Conditions change too fast.
Fatalities can be a crash.

When It Rains
(Progressive)
10/19/2021

When it rains,
Is God crying?
When it rains,
Is someone dying?

Rain water falls,
Drinking in all,
It soaks the ground.
It brings life 'round.

Don't keep tomorrow,
To drown in sorrow.
Do not worry me.
Let the past just be.

Consider this unkind,
Rain brings sadness to mind.
Keep memories heart close,
Of those whom you miss most.

Treasure time that you have shared,
With loved ones you have declared.
Then when memories feel close,
That is what will matter most.

Paradox

(Couplet)

05/01/2021

From a dream I awoke.
In the dark no one spoke.

Something about death,
Makes us take a breath.

The concept cringes creepy,
The feeling deeply eerie.

No one knows the other side.
Is that why we look behind?

Something so unsettling,
The Silence is deafening.

Eyes keep seeking light,
Try to lessen fright.

Hope there's nothing in your head,
That will reawaken dread.

Back to sleeping right?
Try to have good night.

Obsessed
(Couplet)
05/01/2021

More than twelve poems of death,
Am I obsessed?

What is the reason,
For this creepy season?

Why do I write,
Poems of death in the night?

Do they come from my dreams,
Or from some wicked schemes?

From deep in my subconscious,
Does this make me nauseous?

It is the month of May.
Shouldn't I keep these feelings at bay?

This makes thirteen,
A perfect number it seems.

There is no rest,
For a body obsessed.

The Curiosity That Killed the Cat
(Couplet)
09/03/2020

Can you imagine that?
Curiosity killed the cat.

What was this curiosity,
That drove the cat with such ferocity?

Was it the cat's own mind,
That caused it's life to unwind.

Was it human cruelty,
That preyed upon such frailty?

Or was it a fatal feline?
A shrew disdainful and unkind?

Who could this cat be,
Someone like you or like me?

Ominous Predators
(Quatrain)
09/14/2020

The skunk leaves a smell so pungent and rotten,
The stench of it lingers and is not soon forgotten.
It permeates like death so ripe with decay,
It is best to avoid it and flee without delay.

The porcupine sends quills that sting like sharp needles.
You'll wish you had hard shells like beetles,
If seared by them, avoiding pain is feeble,
A million times worse than a hypodermic needle.

Ominous predators exist everywhere.
It's best to avoid them like an attack from a bear.
They lurk within the overgrowth, in the air, and under the
        sea.
They camouflage themselves so the unsuspecting cannot
        see.

Yet the most ominous predator throughout the land
Is the two legged creature known as a human.
With reckless abandon we do unspeakable things
To one another which suffering and despair brings.

NOTE: This poem was written after our dog Ginger got
sprayed by a skunk again.

Water
(Sonnet)
04/07/2021

Is the water kind,
Helping you unwind?
Or do you feel a cloak,
Provoking you to choke?

Does it surround you with ease,
Like a soft gentle breeze?
Or is it cold and wet,
Waiting to steal your breath?

While you quietly lay,
Do you rock and sway?
Or does it pull you down,
Threatening you to drown?

Some love water and its sport.
Some fear it as a last resort.

Driftwood

(Quatrain)
04/07/2021

Driftwood on the shore,
Full of life no more,
Lying here at rest,
Beyond the ocean's crest.

What stories would it tell,
If allowed to dwell,
Among the plants and trees,
Standing in the breeze.

None of life is sure,
Till we breathe no more.
Is this life a test?
Will we find our rest?

Tranquility
(Ballad)
03/04/2021

From the ocean crawl,
With no whine or bawl,
Let the water still,
Feel no longer chill.

Creep along the shore.
Worry you no more.
Lie down on the sand.
Keep your thoughts in hand.

Let your feelings sink.
There's no need to think.
Buried in the sand,
Make no certain plan.

Let the ocean breeze,
Calm your nerves with ease.
Lying on the shore,
Let pain be no more.

As day turns to night,
No more is there fight,
As the setting stills,
Body feels no ills.

John and Jane Doe
(Ballad)
05/01/2021

Two bodies, John and Jane Doe,
Were two people we didn't know.
No more to take a breath.
Just two bodies at rest.

One male, one female body,
Neither one an oddity,
Neither had known the other,
Just lying without cover.

They both appeared young.
So murder this had become.
We had to search out clues,
Before this hit the news.

Now we had to find,
Reasons for their demise.
Dispute there was none.
This was something someone had done.

Death Is Part of Life
(Sonnet)
10/19/2021

Struggling and strife,
Death is part of life.
What is Heaven for?
Somewhere to explore.

Look beyond the door.
Trouble me no more.
I must heed the call,
When the darkness falls.

Don't think I'm obsessed,
Writing about death.
Where we go from here,
We must persevere.

Live life while you can.
Death is in His plan.